Non Finito

poems

Eleanor Swanson

Fernwood
PRESS

Non Finito

Poems

©2022 by Eleanor Swanson

Fernwood Press
Newberg, Oregon
www.fernwoodpress.com

Printed in the United States of America

Cover and page design: Mareesa Fawver Moss

Cover photo: Meritt Thomas via Unsplash

ISBN 978-1-59498-086-2

For Bud, the beloved

Contents

Preface

The poetry in this collection is intended to invite the reader to consider the beauty and vitality to be found in things unfinished, as they are always reminders of what can be finished, as difficult to imagine as that is. The poems focus on the worlds of the seen as well as the unseen worlds, exploring what is real and what is merely fancied. Borrowed from the language of art, "non finito" invokes a fascination with unresolved and open-ended occurrences and events. These poems cover vast terrains, from "unfinished" lives to symphonies, sculptures, and paintings intentionally or inadvertently left unfinished. What did the artists want us to learn or feel? These poems explore this tension.

"Existence is a series of footnotes to a vast, obscure, unfinished masterpiece."

Vladimir Nabokov

I

Epigraph to Feliks in "Non Finito 1" (the principle you've been writing about, *non finito*, evolves best in images from dreams)

Urszula Koziol (translated by W. Martin)

As the Dreamer Waits

While I write poems, my beloved travels.
Today, he is in Kathmandu, sleeping,
dreaming of tomorrow, when he will tour the city.

I imagine his dreams—for my solace and to steal
images for poems. Here is one: He is alone,
walking through the backstreets of the teeming

city and he finds a hidden temple overflowing
with marigolds of the deepest colors only
seen in dreams—vibrant reds and oranges,

flowers he will pick until he has fashioned
a garland he perhaps will wear forever.
Remember, this is a dream and, I, the poet,

produce the place, the scents, the temple,
the blossoms whose petals shine in the sun
as if they had been lacquered for the Buddha.

The waters of a dream flow freely.
In a dream, everything seems as though
it can last forever, trailing through the mind,

evolving, even as the dreamer waits
for the ending that will never come.

Chamber at the End of the Mind

I saw a white pelican floating
in the coolness of the lake
like the swan of dreamtime
with dragonflies flitting beside her—
full of messages about the universe's
rhythms, such as those of the binary
star, Albireo, the head of the swan
in the constellation Cygnus, one
of the forty-eight Ptolemy included
in his famous list of constellations.

I am rinsing my thoughts, asking,
what might succeed grief and how
will I be transformed by sorrow
on this unfinished earth?

The chamber at the end
of the mind has seven rooms
and the seventh and last
is diffused into channels.

Each step becomes a step
into mystery, eternity.

The surface of the lake
is full of clouds.

Heartline

In one corner of the window
a sliver of moon clings
to earth's lighted shadow.

For a long time she listens
to the sound of his breathing,
faint as a wingbeat, or a cricket

rustling grass. She listens
for the uncanny life you hear
in a sleeping person's breathing.

She lifts her hand, stretches
it toward the window.
Two people in darkness.

She holds the moon.
He dreams of snow.
He always dreams

of snow, of walking through
tunnels of snow, of snow caves
blue and silent, of snow drifts,

covering houses to the eaves.
The house is quiet,
but for his soft breathing.

She is far from the singing
and dancing night, from dreams
of laughter and music.

She will open the house, let in
the animal noises of night,
ask him to give words

to the dreams of snow, read
him the meaning of the sickle
moon, curving across her palm,

in a perfect heart line.

Deep in the Willows

Late morning or midday, deep in the willows,
where their larvae feed instar, I have taken many
still photographs of moths, particularly images
of the often nocturnal and sometimes white
or sometimes delicate green Pale Beauty,
Campaea perlata, the color and texture
of the surface on which it alights, leaf, bark,
or blossom, showing through its gossamer wings.

If I acquired more sophisticated equipment,
I would take spiraling moth flight time-lapse
videos, showing moths heading toward
a streetlamp as if it were a distant moon,
first flying in angles toward the light,
then flying in ever-tighter spirals, caught.
It is incomprehensible to see them
so dazzled that they fly until they
are exhausted and fall to their deaths.
I would not like to see my Pale Beauties
so seduced by their own DNA.

How like—and yet unlike—a phenomenon
in space, spiraling subatomic particles
blasted out of photons at nearly light
speed by superconducting colliders.
Spiral motion is the only phenomenon—
the spherical harmonic motion from the
corporeal to nothingness, as if the moths
themselves were moving toward light
at the speed of light, toward the nothing
that is.

I Love You, Says the Heart

We can come to terms with things that can't be
seen and reconcile ourselves to the fact this
need not be tied to a belief in the supernatural.

Who stands behind the door that has just closed?
And from the shards of broken pottery on the asphalt—
can you reconstruct what the jar looked like?
  Or was it a vase?

The air, that phantasmagoric tease, isn't to be
confused with the wind, intimately raking back
our hair or insolently bending trees to its will.
Who wears the shoes with the pattern of radio
waves on their soles?
  And who has seen radio waves?

The difference between things that can
be measured, but never seen, and things
that will never be seen can be understood.
This recognition will lessen our frustration
and cause us to love shadows even
if we sometimes fear darkness.

This isn't a how-to manual; no metaphysical
claims are being made but *absences*
are being described. Absences that resonate
with their own importance—
what the roots of a tree look like, or a seed
swelling in spring-warmed earth, what people
wear beneath their skin, what is really inside
the book under the child's bed.
  What was the message
  in the unopened letter you burned?

What does a quark look like?
It's not meaningful to speak of optical
properties of subatomic particles,
especially components of nucleons.

They'll never be seen, merely believed in,
theorized about. Or the universe itself—
can it be seen? The universe is a fist,
opening and closing like a pulsing heart.

I love you, says the heart, *but you
will never look upon me.*

Flame Vine

Flame vine twists along the fence
like a garland of fire
burning to no end.

Sun, everything is sun,
the green day floating on a bed
of ocean-scented, ocean-damp air.

I am ten and you are five.
With false bravado, I call you "kid."
I swing on the clothes line's

metal T, and you cry
and beg me to lift you.
I say, *Here, let's climb the tree*

instead, and I push you up
the rough bark toward
a lower branch. *Climb out,*

I say, and you do. *Swing,*
I say, and you swing, until
you fall and break your arm.

I am spanked until
the hairbrush snaps in two.
Then I am seventeen and you are twelve.

We sail on water brighter
than the surface of the moon,
dappled with points of flame.

We are lost at sea, desultorily
searching for a green island.
Tacking into the wind, you set

a course that takes us to a rocky
spit of land, we two against
the ocean, swelling and shifting

beneath us, like time itself.
Soon enough, I describe you
to friends, as my handsome brother

grown taller than me, long blonde
hair carried by the wind, you
are sullen and audacious

as the very ocean.
You turn twenty and in July
remodeling a house

an electrical shock
sets your heart vibrating
like a planet sent careening

out of orbit into infinite space.
Your work remained unfinished
and they razed the house.

Until I left this city, I went out of my
way never to pass the lot where your
unquiet spirit might have still lingered.

Dark Photograph

She finds the photograph, 5x7,
black, white, and gray, depicting
three figures in silhouette.
Few details of their faces, their
features, or their clothing can be
made out, though the one in the middle,
a bit shorter than the others, has
long wavy hair, and the one
on the left, hands on hips, elbows
forming triangles the crepuscular
light shows through, wears a cap,
bill turned sideways. Little
is known of the one on the right,
round alien-shaped head melded
with the top of what might be
a spruce tree. Above a faint horizon
line, a gray background is seen,
suggesting mountains or smoke
from a fire billowing out of control.

Who are these people and what
happened when the fire, if it was
a fire, drew closer? Even studying
the photograph carefully, under
magnification, reveals no more
than this.

Three people, outdoors,
whose lives are in danger.

Awakening Captive

ca. 1516–19
Michelangelo Buonarroti, Accademia di Belle Arti, Firenze

How long has he slept inside the marble slab?
The stone Michelangelo knew he would find
in the mountains, in the *pientrasanta* quarry.
The figure writhes and strains
with the effort to awake into life—
to awake into cosmic awareness.
Yet, fixed in stone, we see only an endless struggle
between physical reality and the desire to move
onto another plane of being. The struggle
is primordial, yet eternal. In his state, can we
believe we see incipient recognition of what
his release—never to come—will be like?
His captivity is immortal, but "awakening"
suggests momentum, change, a future.

Here our own pathos of being
is represented—the paradox
of possessing both power
and the vulnerability of nakedness.
We feel the tension between beauty
and vitality and the untamed power
of form, for a sculptor seeing the captive
knows the track of the tools in the stone
shows Michelangelo did not use a flat chisel,
did not seek to polish the captive, to show
him whole. Can one agree with Picasso
that an unfinished work of art "remains

alive, dangerous. A finished work
is a dead work, killed."

Blue Bowl

What are the colors of the hours?
Summer at five a.m. is the blue hour.
The sky, the air, the color of a blue
porcelain bowl, so delicate and thin
you can read through the surface.

At ten o'clock, a breeze sweeps
through the willow and the hour
is thoroughly green if just
for a single moment.

At high noon in late May
I see the colors of Western Tanagers
in flight from tree to tree—brilliant
yellow and red, heads of glossy black.
How quickly they vanish without
disturbing the air, their colors afterimages.

Riffing on sunset at eight: I see tangerine clouds
dappled with pale mauve before they
vanish into twilight gray.

Nine o'clock—
the color of smoke with hints of silver.
Nothing is left except to wait
for nightfall and study black, black,
and silhouettes, and observe the
behavior of inanimate objects.

Elemental

Four ways of apprehending the world
painted in black and white.
Reality creates metaphor;

metaphor creates multiple realities.

I am in my element, light.
Light that, like fire, burns
without consuming.
My companions gather
at each quadrant, outside
the circle, itself quartered,

eternity rendered in a mandala.

Archetype of wholeness,
archetype as muse, individual
conjoined with the archetypal.

What does it mean to be water?
See the shining oval eye of the lake
fixed upon the ever-changing clouds.

Go inside the coveted philosopher's
stone. Even in shadow, there's enough
light to see the Pythagorean
formulas on the walls.

And in shadow the artist has
purified the instinctive part
of the self, with brush strokes
tender, yet certain.

See the forces of nature
manifest here and see first
principles in this ephemeral
reality, indifferent to
everyday life.

In the elemental immerse.

My mind is miraculous,
overflowing with white-hot light.

One-Hundred-Year Storm

I stand on a wooden footbridge that spans
Clear Creek, frothy, rushing water no longer
clear but the color of mud and flecked with bark
and leaves. Sometimes a tree trunk washes past
or strikes the creek's banks with a violent thud.
Towns are islands in the flood, roads have
been washed away, dams fail, thousands
of people have been evacuated.
Boulders roll down hills.

The water rose in the black of night.

Three are dead, and more heavy rain prolongs
the menace as people trudge through rivers of mud.
The trees on the bank twist violently toward
the storm-struck sky, and the pilings of the bridge
tremble as the creek water roars on and on.

We are treading water,

I hear voices say, as though
people are near, watching
me looking out over the current.

This is Armageddon.

Yet it isn't the end of the world, and no
rough beast slouches toward the water-
logged towns and stores and houses.
But later there will be stories,
so many stories of what happened,
what was seen through the curtains of rain
by those who thought they had come
close to eternity.

II

"One should not fear the incomplete, but quite to the contrary, one should deplore that which is too complete. . . . For the incomplete does not necessarily mean the unfulfilled."

Chan Yan Yuan, Tang Dynasty historian

Fragile

She turns corners carefully, not wanting to bump
into a wall. She isn't sick, but grief has made
her feel as if she might easily break and she
wants to stay whole, she wants to feel less
damaged, less sad, and to understand how
her mind and heart might touch, even delicately,
making healing possible, giving her strength
and peace, above all.

    Death is the mother of beauty.

She wants to understand this line
from "Sunday Morning," a poem beginning
with complacencies and ending with extended wings.
What does mother death give birth to?
What kind of beauty? What kind?
She wants to know so she won't break.
Oh, sorrow and desire and the gift of mortality.

    Death is the mother of beauty, mystical.

Mystical as when a human and a creature meet
on a leaf-strewn path in a moment of fragile
communion, both recognizing transience.

    Only the perishable can be beautiful.

She says her heart is breaking, but it isn't broken.
Her sadness will transform itself wholly into love
as the days pass—summer into autumn into winter
into spring and again, again.

Last Light on the West Face of Nanda Devi

For Nanda Devi Unsoeld: 1954–1976

Before the second summit party began the ascent
of the princess of mountains, an ominous black cloud
settled slowly around the summit block, persuading
us to take a rest day, but morale was good.
The next day at seven in the evening, my daughter
Devi was on her last pitch, and it took her until
midnight to haul up over the final lip. A long day.

Two days later, a blizzard kept us in our tents, but
the next morning, Devi was stricken, saying calmly,
"She is calling me. I am going to die," before
she fell into unconsciousness.
I tried to revive her, mouth-to-mouth,
but felt her lips grow cold against mine.
We had lost her. My daughter was gone.
I and the other climbers wept.

Her fiancé Andy and I bundled her in her sleeping
bag and slipped her off the precipice of the North-
East face. I said we had committed her to the deep.

She had been the driving force behind this expedition,
as she was inexorably drawn to her namesake.
The Bliss-Giving Goddess had claimed her own.
An excerpt from her last diary is inscribed
on a stone placed in a high-altitude meadow of Patai:

"I stand on a windswept ridge at night with the stars
bright above and I am no longer alone but I waver
and merge with all the shadows that surround me.
I am part of the whole and I am content."

H. G. Wells Re-imagines Time Travel

When I left my study, an unlit cigar
lay on my desk near the manuscript
I was editing, a tome sure to bring
the critics down on my head.
After pouring myself a glass
of sherry, I returned; the cigar
now rested in a crystal ashtray,
its smoldering tip red as Mars.
Had I traveled through the wormhole
to moments into my future?
And if so, to what consequence?

I am an old man, who regards
The Time Machine as a puerile
work of pseudo-science
and a too-youthful imagination.
Morlocks and Eloi indeed.
Unworthy antagonists.
So…I do not recall lighting
this excellent Havana, but
a single puff tells me it belongs
in this dimension.
Perhaps I am suffering
from dementia, as I approach
the ultimate door to another world.

I hear footsteps in the kitchen.
"Who's there?" I call out,
expecting no one.
Rebecca appears in the doorway,
bearing a tray with five glasses
and a decanter of sherry.
"It's been years since
I've seen you, hasn't it?"
"Not so many, Bertie.
Moura and Constance and
Martha have all come as well."
I laugh. A legion of my lovers
have arrived. Descended?
Near twilight on a late autumn day.
Dare I mention the Tangent universe?
Albert would be appalled.
Ah, no matter. I shall enjoy
these final moments.

Walking Colfax Avenue

In memory of Jake Adam York

It's not quite twilight when I step
from the bus into a crowd of revelers.
The streets are cordoned off,
encircled by yellow tape.
The buses can't go east, so I walk
and walk on, leaving visions behind
me, most disturbingly a joker, and not
the dead Heath Ledger, but one of old—
in yellow and red with a belled hat.
A hand beckons me from a dark
doorway framed by bare wood, leading
into a darker place that more hands—shadowy
hands—wave from, leaving pale vestiges.

I hear a song with a repeating verse,
the singer's voice harsh, then harsher.
But as I walk, the voice drifts away on the wind.
The twilight is deeper now, thick as soup.
I will never be alone on this street, the longest
in the whole of the United States, in the world.
If the universe had streets, well, *non finito*
gifts us with an understanding of infinity.

I am going to a tribute for a poet whose work
was unfinished. His words unravel, becoming
codas enveloped in the unyielding darkness.

Standing Dead Zone: Mount St. Helens

For Harry Truman– died May 18, 1980

He knew the blast of rock,
ash, and gasses was coming.
Soon, molten stone would
flow down the mountain
and into the valley, a force
that would strip trees from hillsides
where he'd walked as a boy,
where he'd walked days ago,
looking for huckleberries.
He'd gathered a basketful.
They were sweet this year.
He knew all about this mountain.
The Indians called it Loo Wa Lat Klah,
"person from whom smoke comes."
He thought of the mountain that way too.

Day after day he saw the magma
swelling the mountain's north flank,
watched the smoke billow up.
He knew the blast was coming.
The intense heat would kill
everything that couldn't hide
in crevices under ice,
but some trees would stand
the ferocious speed of the blast.
They'd stay upright, somehow,
left standing but dead.
What roots they had, those
trees in what they called
the "standing dead zone."
The thought pleased him,
living and dying rooted to earth.

Those who'd come for him—
and there had been many—saw,
finally, that he wouldn't leave,
but they didn't understand.
He was eighty-four.
He'd made a tape with piano
music playing in the background
and the sound of clinking glasses.
His words were simple.
The mountain was part of him.

He was part of the mountain.
The north flank would blow out
and the top of the mountain
would be gone after the blast.
Spirit Lake would fill with mud.
When people remembered,
they'd always say how clear
the water was, how they could
see straight to the bottom.

After the blast, dark smoke
would block the sun.
He and his cats and the lodge
would be buried under mud and ash.
They'd never find him.
He'd be part of the mountain forever.

He'd lived here
all his life and he'd die here, too,
standing, like the trees, still
standing when the blast came,
watching the last morning sun glaze
the valley with dusty light.

The Summer Is an Organism

Days before the solstice, fires rage
through the forests and thick
smoke billows like the clouds
that form the atmosphere
of uninhabitable planets.

Errant campfires, careless
cigarettes, miles of charred
earth, blackened sticks
of trees, and ash falling
in the city, people wearing
masks, anonymous as surgeons
or characters who inhabit
your nightmares, characters
who walk in the night through
the great hole in your mind.

Think of the other dark holes,
the ones the fires are making,
holes in the mind of the sky,
or smoldering deep ravines.
Holes in used party dresses
at the thrift shop, holes
in the shoes of the man
on the corner wearing
camouflage that won't hide
him in a blackened forest
or protect him from enemies,
so he smokes, until gray clouds
billow about his face, like his
own strange planetary atmosphere.

The summer is an organism
creeping through the mind, restless
with heat, showy with flowers
and sunsets with colors never seen
before on this earth, sunsets of fire and ash.

Summer spills over with tragedies—
a dropped match burns a forest
to black rubble; and count in drownings,
poisoned air, and plane crashes—
all cast in images that engrave themselves

on the mind like a landscape struck
white-hot by jagged spears of lightning.

Vestige

Each winter, the boy fell through ice,
playing hockey or skating, or just
walking across Wing Lake in Michigan.
Usually it wasn't hard to pull himself out
of the icy water and crawl up on the ice.

Clothes freezing already, he'd walk home
like that, in his armor of ice, thinking
of the whipping he was going to get
for almost drowning again.

Later, he compared winter,
the season, with the winter
of the spiritual life, the period
of gestation preceding rebirth,
samsara, the eternal cycle
of suffering.

One year, the last he remembered
being on the ice, it broke through
with a loud crack and he dropped
to the bottom of the lake.
The water wasn't deep,
but he was under the ice
for a long time, so long
that he couldn't find the star-shaped
hole he'd made and fallen through.

What he did see, while he was under
the ice, he never described
to anyone, never could describe
that whiff he'd caught, that minute
trace of something numinous,
unnamable, yet forever sought after.

Sketch

A river scene forms slowly in the sketchbook.
The artist today experiments with watercolor.
He has an audience who murmurs about
the sketch, imagining what river the artist
will have depicted when the painting is finished.

They imagine, as he paints, the flowing
rivers of the world—their thoughts are busy
with images of their own. The Li, a tributary
of the Yangtze. The Loire. The Colorado.
The Nile. The Ganges. The Irrawaddy.
The Amazon; the thinkers are beguiled
by what they believe they will see
as details emerge with each brushstroke.

They dream while awake of hippo pods,
ancient temples, funeral ghats, the Valley
of Kings, mountains, grand chateaus,
the planet alive with each flowing river,
each with its own capacious heart.

The painter paints light. Light and shadow.
Warm reflected light, sky light, direct light.
He himself has drifted into the flowing
waters of a dream, tangled in half-formed
images. The uber-river flows silently
through his mind.

Never Developed

I hold the 4x6 negative up to a lamp
rotating it carefully between thumb
and forefinger, keeping it clean,

free of smudges, seeing the reversed
blacks and whites, some images
in gray, intensity of contrast—a black

wedding dress and dainty shoes, dark
sky, a gray and black bouquet, the bride's
mouth—sorrowfully—a black hole.

I put the negative first on white paper
then black, daring not to caress the film's
shiny surface. Dear bride, wedding party

in tones of smoke and ash, did you see
either the light or the shadow or both?
The ceremony was all over before

it started, and nothing can be fixed.

Into the Enchanted Dark

You hear a shattering, see
a star wheeling down, burning
out through layers of air and dust.

When morning sunlight drizzles
through bare branches, you dream
of dancing, stepping high.

A jig it was.

You breathe. Breathe. And stop.
Surprised at the last.

Goodbye earth that I love.
I wasn't finished here.

They call you by name,
but now you are girl of the air,
unworldly and untitled.
You look below to see your mourners,
their faces silver with tears.
You are borne into the wind.

You dance!

Miles above the ground,
floating beyond the sorrowful drone
of the pipes, you watch as your black
slippers drop and drift away.
You trail a yard of lace.
Rings fall from your fingers.

The geese fly far below you, crying,
over the ready, open grave.
Nine and fifty carriages line
the avenues.
Rose petals drift down, feather-
slow to rest on earth.

You read the characters of sky
and cloud, the needles of dwindling
sun, you read the deepening light,
studying each sublime message
until you understand.
You are the beloved girl of air,
dissolving into the invisible,
disappearing into the enchanted dark.

The Pond

If you sit close to the edge
of the pond, you can watch
an early wind rise up and ripple
the water's surface.
After a while, an hour perhaps,
all will grow still, the wind
gone, the pond's dark surface
smooth as an obsidian plate.

If you are there near noon,
the pond will gleam with points
of light, and later you can see
the reflection of the camellia
trees and the Japanese maples.
Sometimes camellia petals
are scattered along the pond's
sandy edge or, having drifted
from the tree, float on the pond's
surface, small pink boats holding
tiny mesh web spiders and drops of dew.

As you walk around the pond,
don't miss seeing the resurrection
fern growing out of the tallest
of the water oaks.
Don't slip and fall into the water.
The pond is deep, much deeper
than anyone could imagine
and full of legends, even bodies
perhaps, I've been told.

Once near twilight, someone sitting
at the pond's edge, as you might be
now, believed he saw something
ghostly in the pond. Frightened,
he turned and walked away feeling
a heaviness with each step he took,
seeing, in fact, the deep impression
of each footprint in the sand as he
turned his back upon the pond,
never to return.

The Day Jerry Garcia Died

For Bob

We were driving down Washington Street
in Miami Beach, having just passed a man
wearing a four-color whirligig hat.
An offshore wind lifted his long wispy
gray hair—bad for surfers.

I flipped on the radio and heard the news:
"Sadly, for his legions of fans, Jerry
Garcia's long, strange trip came to an end
today in a California rehabilitation
facility, where it is thought he died
of a heart attack." I looked at my husband.
"We've got to call Bob," he said, Bob,
a true Deadhead, who wrote a poetry
collection about The Grateful Dead,
would already be in mourning,
as if he'd just lost a member
of his family, which, in a way, he had.

Unlike Bob, I'd never been a true
fan, perhaps because a former
friend of ours played "Ripple"
at every social gathering we'd
ever had—her fingers struggling
to find the chords quickly enough,
her eyes closed as if she were
enraptured, her thin voice singing
the words—"A ripple in still water/
when there is no pebble tossed/
nor wind to blow." *Ah, that's deep,*
was the cruel thought I had.

But for Bob, "Ripple" was the song
that filled the air for him.
Back at the hotel we called
with our condolences. "Poor
fucker," Bob said, through tears.
"Last time I saw him his
voice was gone. He served
the music," Bob said sorrowfully.
"I would sit Shiva for him if I could."

III

"Dark things tend to brightness/Bodies fade out in a flood of colors, /Colors in music, so disappearing is the destiny of destinies." Eugenio Montale, former president of the Academy of American Poets (translated by Jonathan Galassi).

The Astronomy Book

I took the astronomy book from the shelf—
the one I bought on our first anniversary
to teach my husband the stars.
Light rolled off the slick pages.
The gray italic print of formulas,
galactic dust impressed there.
I thumbed through suns and solar
systems, remembering the point
of my search: some star I wanted
to pluck out of the book to bring
on darkness and the glitter of the moon,
further spreading the farmer's brash
white floodlights over the rutted fields.
Outside together, I follow your arm,
pointing to the sky, pointing out
a star, as you tell your colorful story
of its discovery, and how it must
have winked out millennia ago.
You send shivers up my spine
as I thought of interstellar dust
and matter adrift. You school me—
from hottest to coldest, the seven main
groups of stellar spectra—OBAFGKM.

Oh be a fine girl, kiss me.
And I did, standing under
the faint light of millions of stars.

Pablo Neruda's Holiday

All he wished for was a brief respite—
a day saturated in the water's most intense
azul and his first memory, his first breath.

What sea were you near, Neruda, and what
were you singing, as you wrote in green,
your color of hope? Did you watch
the vowels you loved "leap like silver fish"
and then catch them midflight?

On his holiday, Pablo Neruda swims
steadily out to sea, singing.
The water laps his chin.
His strokes are strong and smooth
as he listens for someone, something,
spelling his name.

He sings "light is like water,"
and when he stops singing
he realizes he has begun
to compose a song
for a *festival de canción española*—
a song for *la raza*, a song
for multitudes.

Extinction: Painted

She paints the shape of a bird as empty
space, showing through to nothing,
neither past nor future, yet the painter
must give nothing a color, so nothing
is pink and shining and hard as quartz,
unfeathered, yet a perfect outline of
the orange-headed green and yellow
Carolina parakeet, now gone from
the earth since Inca died in the Cincinnati
Zoo more than ninety years ago.
"Once you get a celebrity cage and
a human name," reads the painter's caption,
"your species is done for." The Carolina
parakeet became extinct for the usual
reasons: hunting by humans being foremost.
"The Parakeets," wrote Audubon, "are destroyed
in great numbers. The farmers' guns at work,
killing ten or even twenty at every discharge."

The painter stretches her canvas to start
another painting, heartbroken, yet
curious to choose from a new extinct
animal each week; which to paint?

Black Rock by the Sea

At Playa Samara, Costa Rica,
a woman climbs up a black rock.
The rock's smooth surface
is slippery with sea water.
Between the beach and Isla Chora
is a reef, good for snorkeling.
The reef swarms with bright fish
such as neon-blue damselfish
and three-banded butterfly fish.

The sun has just set.
Fierce pink and golden light
streaks the sky horizontally,
starkly contrasting with
the now-gray water,
gnashed with white surf.

Tomorrow is the first day
of August. She feels herself
trying to balance but not yet
balanced between one
kind of time and another.
Sunset and night.
Late summer and fall.

The stars will soon appear
one by one as the sky darkens.
When she steps down from the rock,
slowly, so as not to slip, her bare
feet will meet sand and a wind
will come up, bringing the sea
closer and also the faint scent
of the birds of paradise flowers
bordering the beach hotels.

This scent brings drama
and wreathes her, if only
tenuously, in pleasure.

Bella

I was walking on the shoulder of the road
that runs next to the cemetery, when I saw
a woman standing near the cemetery fence,
looking at a monument—a black granite
heart with a stone angel draped across it.
She stood quite still for a moment,
but then began to weave her way
among the placid stones and markers.

She started calling out, "Bella, Bella!"
her voice pitched high, her face wearing
an anguished look. A lost child, I thought
at first, but then the name and a command,
"Come, Bella. Come." She was in Woodlawn
Cemetery looking for a lost dog.
What happened, I wondered, as she walked
further among the gravestones, still calling,
calling. Instinctively, I scanned the gully
between the road and the cemetery boundary,
fearing the worst. But I saw no dead dog,
just refuse, soda and beer cans, cigarette
butts, fast-food wrappers, leaves, and twigs.

My heart was heavy with the thought of Bella,
as the woman's cries grew fainter, and she grew
smaller as she disappeared in the lush green
of the trees, among the dead, today, only the dead,
no one visiting loved ones, no workers,
no one in the cemetery but the grief-stricken
woman, looking for her lost dog.

Watching the Water

What do they see, those who come
to the lake and stand, or sometimes sit
on the wooden benches at the lake's
sandy edge? They stare, men and
women, young and old, and they
do not appear to be contemplating
the lake's dazzle or looking for anything
in particular, such as the mallards
and their ducklings or the cormorants
drying their dark, slightly ominous wings,
or the swallows sweeping the water's surface.

Their stillness and fixed expressions
are disquieting, making me think
of things outside the known world.

The watchers seem to be memorizing
the water and hoping in turn that the water
will remember them, so that when they
next come to the lake, they won't have
to expend so much time, so much effort.

Those who watch the water know that,
like the mind, the lake is wider than the sky.

Sometimes I come back at twilight
and find a few of the watchers still
standing at the lake's edge, silhouetted
against the sky, still memorizing
the water and hoping the water
will remember them.

Perhaps they see mirrored in the lake
the world on fire—pestilence, death,
famine, suffering of all kinds, endless war.
Perhaps they sometimes also see
beauty beyond description.

When they finally turn away from the lake,
they walk in the growing darkness—
thinking they are heading home at last—
but they are no longer sure it is the right way,
the right place, anymore, to be.

Archaeology

Shards of pottery are like letters
that, put together, form a sound,
human cries like *oh* or *ah* or *I am.*
Other syllables are added to surprise.
She digs more deeply into the earth,
deeper and deeper to find more layers.
Here is a spoon, here is a spent bullet.
She makes a story out of these two things.

Then, hungry to form more words, she
starts with breathing, inhaling, exhaling,

>*Aspire, conspire, sublimate.*
>*Sentience, transience.*

She is a transient, hungry to form words,
to taste them as smoky, as sweet, to roll
them in her mouth until they no longer
have rough edges but are smooth
as stones that rest in eons of oceans.

Silver light is everywhere,
ancestors floating through
their half-lives, ambitiously
circling furniture and trees.
Time is pregnant, and then
it gives birth and allows
its infants to float among
both the living and the dead.

A flock of migratory birds, white
shapes against the pale tissue-blue
sky turn and wheel as one force, high
above the rolling green prairie grass.

Breathe. And again.
Let sublimation carry you
from one world to the next.

This Day in History, September 2

On this day in history, the first ATM installed
in America starts dispensing cash at Chemical
Bank in New York City, and the last *Star
Trek* episode airs, "Requiem for Methuselah."
Poor Rayna. Kirk's android fetish strikes again!
World War II ends and Ho Chi Minh declares
Independence from France, and soon, French
warships start to bomb Haiphong.

The Republic of Grasshoppers has ceased
to reign but bees are still buried deeply
in the spires of purple verbena.
The foxtails have burst into stars.

A major typhoon hits the city of Hong Kong.
A large Italian Cruise Liner was picked up
during the typhoon like a stick and tossed on shore.

Someone writes about mountains of snow,
more snow than she has ever seen in her life.
Someone else asks questions he doesn't
know the answers to, mostly questions
about woolly worms, brown recluses,
and Van Gogh's twelve paintings
of sunflowers (no hothouse beauties!)
in a newly invented yellow pigment.

Today, somewhere, there is levity,
and a man in black, who's just
gotten off the bus, walks east.
An interloper tries to decide whether
the world is ephemeral or liminal.

The Harley Davidson turns 100.
A Mammoth skull is found in France.
George Gershwin signs his name
to the finished score of Porgy and Bess,
calling it "his masterpiece."

A flock of white pelicans fly
in formation, their feathers
and black wing tips patterning
the light gray sky as they glide
in circles before descending
onto the lake.
Two swallowtail butterflies
finish the day in an amorous dance.

Before midnight, a woman dreams
of falling and then rising again,
changed, utterly changed.

Summer of the Hawks

In the spring we saw a pair
of Cooper's hawks, tiercel and hen,
high in our neighbor's Catalpa tree,
long before its white blossoms appeared.
The hawks were mostly silent then, brooding
in the uppermost branches of that tall tree
or sometimes flying together, diving
and gliding over other treetops.

But then the chicks came, and soon
they were fledglings, and Catalpa petals
were floating down and carpeting
the street our aerie of hawks flew over,
high and low, their calls half a cry, half
a whistle—cries for food, feeding cries,
call and response, all day long.
Sometimes they flew from the Catalpa
to the enormous dead elm, skeletonous,
in our front yard, or they perched on
the utility pole in our backyard above
the bird feeder I hoped was well-concealed
by overhanging branches of the plum tree.

More than once I've stood, watching
a perched hawk gazing down
unflinchingly at me—a mere mortal.

The neighbor across the street calls
out as we both stand in our front yards.
"They're teaching the young to kill,"
he says, and then, he amends,
"to hunt." He laughs uncomfortably.

When we walk the dogs, we pass
clusters of feathers—doves, flickers,
and more—fanned out on the grass,
no other traces of their lives.

In the back, a tall branch
in the apple tree points upward
in a Y shape, a perfect perch where
the finches often sit. I want to tell
them, *Danger, fly away.*

This afternoon, some chickadees are at the feeder
and some are deep in the trees, calling *dee,*
dee, dee, wanting more seeds.

I watch that high branch where a rosy finch
now sits. I watch for the flash of wings—
beautiful and terrible too—
and the tiny bird, vanished.

My Mother's Ghost

The long twilight of Swedish summer
keeps us talking late into the evening.
The ghost of my mother has joined
the gathering of relatives.
She sits on a hard chair, the twilight
blue of the sky flowing into the room,
itself more a ghost light than her own.

Her legs are crossed, and the glitter
of lamplight is caught in her glasses.
Then she taps one foot on the floor.
Her hands lie demurely in her lap.
She is watching my father,
patiently waiting to be noticed.
Her white hair has been cut, styled,
and tinted a daring, dusky rose.

The furrows of pain and confusion
have vanished from her forehead.
She has gotten back her good dress
from the church rummage sale,
the gauzy one with a wildflower print.
Her dark shoes are sturdy and new,
and have the sheen of fine leather.
She wears a white orchid
in her hair and keeps tapping
her right foot, a little louder
and faster now, as the relatives
talk only to my father and don't
seem to notice her at all.

I lean forward in my chair, hoping
to be caught in her blue gaze,
thinking perhaps of interrupting
on her behalf, glancing for a moment
at my father taking a bite of cake.

When I look back, she's gone,
having stepped onto the balcony
where she can listen unseen
to how her life's evoked,
where she can fly away in the guise
of a sparrow whenever she wishes.

I Set Them Aright

That stifling day at Cape Sable,
horseshoe crabs lay rotting
in the sand, strewn like refuse.
The dead creatures,

the stinking seaweed, the ruined pier,
all pointed to the end of something.
Not the end of the world—not yet.
Nor the end of the horseshoe crabs.

After 200 million years, after
creeping among dinosaurs
and regarding with their double eyes
the last mastodon falling away to bone,

they won't soon pass into extinction.
Harmless, they neither sting nor pinch,
but who would want them anyway—
homely, inedible things who've outlived

the dodo and passenger pigeon,
giant hog, and woolly mammoth,
and thousands more extinctions.
I right a carapace with a stick.

They have survived enough history
to deserve more dignity in death than this—
rotting among the swarming flies and mosquitoes,
swept ashore near some long-abandoned homestead.

They will outlive me—*Limulus polyphemus.*
I set them all aright, in a line
that will wash them out to sea
with the next tide.

IV

"[The unconquerable form of matter] truly is all that it can be; and so it has all measure, has all species of figures and dimensions in the aesthetic realm of the unfinished." Giordano Bruno in *Cause, Principle, and Unity*

A Man Tries His Hand at
Building a Flagstone Path

He carries a level and a measuring tape,
looking closely at each piece of flagstone before
he places it in the hard clay that he's been trying
to smooth out for days, running his backhoe
over it again and again, *scrape, beep, beep,*
and repeat, repeat, fraying his nerves to thin
wires that would give off sparks if they touched.
He lays a stone, then another, moving them closer
with his shoe, as if that would work. Intractable
stone on clay, hard as the stone itself. The path
begins to curve toward a driveway, and then
he makes a spiral. Perhaps he is thinking maze
or labyrinth or nebula. The temperature
has climbed into the nineties. The man sweats,
steps back, and looks at the path, the spiral.
He looks long and hard, and again pushes
one stone toward another with the toe of his boot.
Then he walks up a stone step onto his unfinished
deck, and sits in a chair, seeming to stare at the street.
His hands dangle between his knees; his jaw goes slack.
He imagines that the path, if finished, would take
him somewhere, out into the vast universe
perhaps, or at least out of the cauldron heat,
take him away from his unspeakably futile task.

Crossing Over

Voices from the house
rise and fade on the wind.
The yellow lamplight
grows dimmer as she walks

farther into the woods.
Hummingbirds whir by,
taking her for something newly
hatched, helpless in darkness.

She finds her way
through trees,
feeling the tall grass cling
to her clothes, then pull

free with a harsh whisper.
The murmur of night
fills her. Everything alive
breathes at once.

She hears a horse's sigh
before she sees him, long flanks
shining in moonlight.
She runs her hands along his cool neck.

Her fingers sift through the rough mane.
He snuffles and steps closer
pawing dirt.
She imagines climbing

onto him and galloping away,
into the empty night.
She rode bareback once, until
the horse slipped from her

and she fell onto a cinder path.
When she was conscious again,
she could remember nothing.
Was she even alive?

She's alone with the past.
The horse whinnies softly
as if readying her for a ride
in the tearing wind,
over miles of rough land,
a course of flesh before
bones, the infinite future before
the present, to the pasture's end.

Sounds to Bring the Heart and Mind Together

"How can I invent when I sing?"
Pablo Neruda

A blue heron flies above against
the deeper blue sky, its shape
momentarily forming a four-
stroke *kanji*, the Japanese
character for "water."

水

Then the wings no longer
form a word as the heron
glides into shade and hides
in the gray bank shadows
of the lake.

Scores of barn swallows
soar, then descend in wavering
diagonals across a busy intersection,
swooping low, near missing
shining windshields and the red
apex of the traffic light.
The light turns green. I move
through the soar and glide—
the tinted air.

In a barn with walls of summer air,
I see the gleam of the swallows' eyes.
Their breast down floats near-invisible,
like tiny puffs of brown smoke.

I want to see an eagle on my way
to the next world. I want to know
what those eyes, that beak,
that eight-foot wingspan
mean in this world.

If eagles could sing, they
would be Tuvan overtone
throat singers, looking for
the right river to fly over,
mimicking nature's sounds
to bring the heart and mind together.
Finches sing in a minor key,
and meadowlarks rise straight
up from the tall weeds, singing,
like the presumed ascent of ghosts,
angels, spirits, name your truth.

Prey found, the hawk sings,
allegro cry.

Meadowlark glissandos
we can listen to
for light years echo
through the tall grass.

Landmine Museum

Siem Reap, Cambodia

I walk down the leaf rot clay
path toward bells, flutes, soft
drumming, sound traveling
in waves, as light falls
through the gum trees.
Khmer music.
I stand before the band
of men—one blind and others
missing legs, faces unflinching
as the temple bas-reliefs.

Many landmines are still buried
in the outlying forests.
The men play halfway
between the road and the temple—
Ta Prohm. Serenity unflinching.

Frogs screech in the river.
Strangler fig and silk-cotton tree roots
snake down through and among
ancient stones and *devatas*—
female deities—and wind
into the Hall of Dancers.
The tops of the trees rest
on towers and the walls
of the inner moat, abundantly green.

Temple and trees have grown
together in fragile symbiosis.
Down the road, near Banteay Srey
Temple, is the Landmine Museum.

Next to the many types of landmines
on display are drawings
of the fighting during the war.
Next to the house is an artificial mine
field, showing how the mines
have been hidden in the jungle.
We meet some of the landmine
victims the curator of the museum
has adopted into his family.
Before we leave, we make
a contribution and take further reading
with us about the fields, still killing fields,
the dark, rich earth holding
the mines in an unspeakable embrace.

Remnants of Buried Lives

The path is a narrow strip of gray dirt—
rocks, pebbles, bits of foil and glass,
white and green, shining
like worthless gems.

At a curve, foxtails bow over the path.
Days ago, after rain, the path
was mud, and someone rode
a horse whose hooves left
deep grooves in the path.
They hardened to craters
and shadows pooled in them.
The hoof prints had no pattern.
Maybe the rider reigned in
her mount and the horse reared,
balked, and high-stepped
from side-to-side in the muck.

The days grew drier and the craters
turned to ruts, and then handprints
appeared, palm up.
The rain ceased altogether
until a thousand footfalls
pounded the path flat again.

Grasshoppers couple and uncouple
and leap into the waist-high weeds.
The path is like a teeming city,
except quieter and purer.

People sometimes leave things
on the path, blood of unknown
origin, gloves, socks, and keys.
At different times, over many
years on the path, I have found

two silver wedding rings, one
small and one large.

Shadows sometimes stretch
across the path, like loosely
woven shawls.

Cobblestones lie half-buried
in the path, remnants of ancient cities.
Remnants of buried
lives that will remain
eternally unknown to us,
except in troubling elegies.

My Name is Rupa

In April, I sat at my sewing machine
holding the yoke of a shirt, a Wrangler,
mixed colors, a plaid fabric. I ran a seam.
It takes two hands to make a shirt, sure
hands, no hesitating, for the bosses
want the work done fast.
My mother stood near me saying
we'd take breakfast together.
We both worked in Rana Plaza.
She made shorts and I made shirts.

Later, in the building's rubble,
they'd find labels and piles of
unfinished clothing—C & A,
Benetton, Mango, Primack, Cato.

The factory floor rolled beneath
my feet. My mother vanished.
That morning, we'd seen cracks
in our building, but were told
to enter or we would not be paid.

I dropped the unfinished shirt and ran
through thick dust, screaming, *save me.*
I am alive. I am here. I am Rupa!

The Garden

Roses in profusion, you said, and stone benches
in shade where one can sit and read on cool afternoons.
Trellises trailing ivy, leaves shiny green and dappled.
You produced drawings—four at least—and quoted
from Marvell, saying the garden would be a place where
"sweet and wholesome hours/Be reckoned but with/
herbs and flowers." And a fountain would spill
onto a streambed bordered by native stone.
The final drawing was a rendering in color.

You ordered the roses—Wild Edric, a beautiful rugosa.
You read from the catalog: "A Wild Edric hedge
will quickly become completely impenetrable,
with the many prickly stems displaying gorgeous,
textured foliage." *Impenetrable*. I pondered that word,
in its many senses, from the mind to the rose hedge.

I think of the garden, what it will be, the roses
planted, the vines clawing their way up the trellis.
Impenetrable. I can't shake those five syllables,
ironically tempting me to enter a place
I can never enter.

My love, your thoughts have become impenetrable.
Impossible to understand. Inscrutable.

I wonder at the fact that Alexander Marvell
has become your favorite poet.

You wander the place that will become
the garden carrying a slim volume
of his words, reading aloud:
"Fair quiet, I have found thee here,
And innocence, thy sister dear!
Society is all but rude to this delicious solitude."

Not admitting impressions on the mind.

The roses came, but when you planted them,
it was mid-July and they didn't flourish in the heat.
The vines—you wanted ivy—seemed
unhappily to claw their way up the trellis,
full of penetrable spaces.
Sometimes I sat on a folding chair, under
a little spruce that had long been in the back
yard, remembering that someone once said
of Marvell, that he was a butterfly, turned caterpillar.

Preventing another body from occupying the same space
at the same time.

Not to be impressed in mind or heart.

The garden. I sit in its ruins waiting for miraculous
growth, fecundity, for the world to become literal again.
I wait, distant lover, for days of sowing and planting
in your good company.

Rain

Rain has fallen every day for sixteen days, heavily at times,
torrential. The sun has been out a total of five minutes and
during this time, looked at worshipfully.
Now the sky is the color of tarnished silver, a flat, tedious
color, wanting for pinpricks of blue or even rolling dark
thunderheads to break up such monotony.
At this moment, it isn't raining, but the forecast says more
to come, every day. Henceforth? Not a Biblical word but late
Old English, dating from the 14th century.
Flood warnings abound, water laps over roadways, pastures
and lawns, soaked. Oh, for want of sun, what have people done
about being deprived of light?
They turn on lights in every room, look at holiday photographs
and bright paintings, find music that reminds them of sunlight
dappling fields and woods, sleep longer than usual hoping
they'll awake to blue skies, chide themselves for their lack
of resilience, keep meticulous journal notes on their feelings.
This is not a catastrophe, these days of rain—not a 100-year
storm, hurricane, earthquake, tsunami, forest fire, mass
extinction, nuclear plant meltdown.
People take out their umbrellas and walk their dogs
(though the dogs tremble). They put on raingear and run
through the neighborhood, around the overflowing lakes.
But these days make people susceptible to loneliness,
although they are not alone, to phobias, although
they have nothing to be afraid of, to languor,
even while awake, to a draining of passion,
to dyspepsia, loss of appetite, inability to laugh heartily,
and to a host of other senseless, imagined ills
as they check the weather reports daily.
The tiniest patch of blue sky is heartening, even
though it is only seen for minutes before the clouds
cover it over with impunity, insolence, indifference.

Rain begins to fall again, just a few drops at first, then
spatters; then a veil of hard rain is all there is to be seen,
no trees, no grass, no spring flowers.
You want to know now, how this ends, how many
more days pass, how long before the afternoon darkness
descends, whether this story
is endless. how many more words will be exchanged
about the rain.
The story ends today, with glorious
sunlight and warmth, guaranteeing everyone's happiness,
for a while, at least. Indeed.

Refraction

Last October the light on the trees
intensified the reds, yellows,
and golds, even the fading green—
for the whole month, it seemed.
This October, after four hard frosts,
most of the leaves have fallen, but
the leaves on the maples still flame
red as custom sport's car red, red
as an image from an illuminated manuscript—
so red, as if it's not ever quite going
to be winter, and harvest hasn't started,
and Halloween and masks and disguises
won't ever come, and they'll be no
heavy curtains of falling snow, no
blinding snowstorms, nothing rooting
at my heart with the mind of winter.

Leaves twirl down in a light wind,
and someone stops—a woman
on the sidewalk outside my window
stops to pick up a handful of maple leaves.
She bends down for a long time,
taking pleasure, it seems,
in collecting just the right leaves.

Such richness lies in the moment,
my watching her unseen, as
the leaves fall gently around
her, some catching in her hair.

Light refracts from everything,
each with its own angle of incidence—
the mottled tree bark, the surface
of leaves, windshields, the aggregate,
the sand, the shimmer of mica,

the light post, the still-green blades
of grass, the colored gravel border,
the glossy hair of babies, the squirrel's
flicking tail, my own pen, scratching
the paper, my decades-old wedding ring.

October was when we met, costumed,
disguised, at Halloween, Quasimodo
and Amelia. The makings of my
masquerade were too vague for you
to know I was the famous Earhart,
but I understood that your hump
was emblematic of pain.

Later that night, the snow
falling around us, glowing
in the light of the party house,
we kissed, not remembering
it was October, being for
the moment, no longer conscious
of anything but the snow falling
silently and our embrace.

Reverend Blair Talks about Copernicus

For Tipton

Suddenly Reverend Blair said, dramatically—
"Cosmology, the vastness of space
and a single human life lost. A world
now less secure and comfortable. Copernicus.
The sun is the center." Where was he going,
I wondered. Was this a mere digression?
A play on words? A metaphor?

Reverend Blair paused and bowed his head.
Was he praying? The pause grew long.
Collectively, we waited in the silent church.
The reverend raised his head and finally spoke.
"A diaphanous delusion was what his critics
said about the earth's rotation around the sun."
David would have understood, he assured us.
We knew of David's passionate
interests: astronomy, mathematics,
and football, perhaps not in that order.
"The spirit opens as life closes down, and
so Copernicus published *On the Revolutions
of the Heavenly Bodies* as he lay
on his deathbed. As we bid our son
David goodbye, we will remember
that *he* lay on his deathbed
with courage."

Afterward, outside the sanctuary in stark
late fall sun, we saw more clearly
the reverend's big white teeth, decidedly
unministerial, instead theatrical
or false perhaps, gleaming in the light.
During the eulogy, he'd smiled a lot,
especially between each of his

many digressions—one about football,
a game our friend David loved;
another about his own dead son, and more.
Reverend Blair no longer seemed the same
man who had just talked about heliocentric
theory and death. Had this been theater
or had the man gone mad, channeling
Nicolaus Copernicus?
We only knew that—for a moment—
the sun blazed and earth stood still.

Synesthesia

What is to be made of that curious and rare
crossing of the senses? Synesthetes
can "hear" colors, "smell" sounds,
or perceive words and numbers
in different hues, shapes, and textures.
Ah, E-sharp is blue, and the month
of March is quartz-pink like the bud
of a spring flower or a deep breath.
"Thy visible music blasts make deaf
the sky," wrote Keats in a synesthetic
image-making frenzy, almost besting
Shakespeare's "trumpet-tongued blast."

I plunge my hands into the silver snow
and feel that brightness, that shine run
through my veins, fingertips to brain
cobwebbed with the patched colors
of dreams. Brain to the heart's lotus
all silver, through my gut, *silver* I hear
you in my toes, in each step.
As the silvery fingers of pure
cold sweep through me, "I long
for a beaker of the warm South."

Imagine a jazz ballad shimmering
over the heads of a coffee-shop
crowd like an iridescent watercolor.

Awake! How do you know but
"ev'ry Bird that cuts the airy way
is an immense world of delight,
clos'd by your senses five?"

Isaac Newton on the Playground

At the King's School, I carved my name
on the wall, as was customary at the time.
I was twelve when I began my studies
there, an education that commenced
when I was seventeen and ready
to enter Trinity College in Cambridge.
I have no memories of those early
years at King's save one, when I
and the other lads played in the courtyard
on a windy summer day and in my
head I timed the gusts of wind,
outleaping all of my bigger, hardier
playmates. I could see on each
face surprise and embarrassment.
Inwardly smiling, I continued
to study the force of moving air,
matching my fascination with time.

I have lived long without forgetting
how I leapt up and up, a scrawny boy
exhibiting strength of will and mind.
Now I have grown old and am revered
like a god who is often asked how
I made my discoveries. I reply with
disinterest: "Truth is the offspring
of silence and unbroken mediation."

Reading the Runes

Older ones are written on scraps
of yellowed paper folded like
letters that will never be mailed.
Some recent ones have been
written in the kitchen and bear
unsavory, unrecognizable stains.
Some are dumb in the sense they
will never speak again, and in
the other sense—full of false
grandeur, silly notions, abstract
weightless ideas, wrong words.

On many unfinished poems
the hopeful poet has written
copious notes to herself about
how the poem must be revised:
add a word here; this is a terrible
title. What does it mean? Here
is the key stanza. Why is it
buried in the middle of the poem?

Some of the notes are questions,
but the poet is scolding
the unfinished poem as well.

Most of these works-in-progress
will always be in progress,
because the poet doesn't have
the sense to know when to stop.

Those writers who stop in the middle
of a line presage a failure of nerve,
breath, or pure ennui.

The words, the gaps, quenched
flame—all must be read like runes.

One Wonderful Sunday

Shomin-geki
After Akira Kurosawa

"You can't eat dreams," he says to her smiling face,
as they watch orphans picking through trash
in the rubble of Tokyo. "But you can *have* dreams,"
she insists, after a visit in a driving rain to a model
home they can't afford. He finds her constant
optimism absurd. Spirits can be broken irreparably.

"We'll go the Schubert concert after all." Unfinished, he thinks.
Number 8. Unfinished things lead only to disillusionment
and despair, depression, life perpetually played out
in a minor key. Yet he follows her to the band shell trailing
along behind her, feeling mocked by her liveliness of spirit.
Of course they find it empty, hollow as a giant bivalve.
She takes a seat in front and cocks her head, a hand
behind one ear, listening, her eyes bright.

"Oh, how lovely and mysterious," she says. "There is a ghost.
What happened to him? Why didn't Schubert finish his symphony?"
So many questions, he thinks, but he answers mildly. "Perhaps
he fell ill, or simply got bored with his work. So as for the ghost,
We'll never know." Two movements, Allegro moderato
and Andante con motto, B minor, D759, thought lovely
by some critics and quite odd by others. Putting his cynicism
aside for a moment, because he himself loves
Schubert, he will try to participate in her charade.
Suddenly, she stands up. "Please," she says, gesturing
toward the stage. "Please." She takes a knitting
needle from her bag and offers it to him, his baton.

Half-heartedly he climbs on stage and begins
to mime conducting, not even imagining
an orchestra or a single musician sitting before him.
She applauds and stands again, clapping loudly.
When she is seated, he continues to wave his "baton."
Moments pass as he conjures Schubert composing
this fragment of a symphony, and as these thoughts
arise, he begins to hear the first movement note-by-note.
Something breaks free in him. The music is real.
He has been absorbed, out-of-time, into Schubert's world.

He does not know how long he conducts, rain
dripping from his hair, as he gives in to his wild heart.
Finally, he bows low, in the Japanese way.
His beloved companion rises once again,
and begins to clap and clap until
the sound echoes magisterially
through the band shell, filling the emptiness.

Acknowledgments

Thanks are due to the editors of the following publications in which these poems first appeared:

Cargo Literary: "Disturbance of Surfaces"

Chiron Review: "Sketch"

Driftwood Press: "Chamber at the End of the Mind"

Compose Journal: "I Love You, Says the Heart"

Exit 13: "Pokhara"; "This Day in History, September 2"; "Landmine Museum"

Homestead Review: "The Astronomy Book"; "Flame Vine"

Interdisciplinary Studies in Literature and the Environment: "Standing Dead Zone"; "The Summer is an Organism"; "One-Hundred-Year Storm"; "Deep in the Willows"

Steam Ticket: "Awakening Captive"

The Missouri Review: (featured), "As the Dreamer Waits"; "Dark Photograph"; "Blue Bowl"; "Crossing Over"; "Vestige"

Inverted Syntax: "Watching the Water"; "Elemental"; "Walking Colfax Avenue"

Bosque Press: "Fragile"

The Cape Rock: (forthcoming), "Never Developed"

Apeiron Review: (forthcoming), "Last Light on the West Face of Nanda Devi"

Duck Lake Journal: (forthcoming), "The Pond"

The Wayne Literary Review: (forthcoming), "My Name is Rupa"

About the Poet

Eleanor Swanson is a widely published poet and fiction writer who holds a PhD from the University of Denver. Her poems have been featured twice in *The Missouri Review*. Her work has appeared in the *Southern Review*, *Black Warrior Review*, the *Denver Quarterly*, the *Bloomsbury Review*, the *American Poetry Journal*, and in many other notable publications. Awards include an NEA Fellowship. She has been nominated three times for a Pushcart Prize. Her first poetry collection, *A Thousand Bonds: Marie Curie and the Discovery of Radium*, won the Ruth Stevens Award (NFSP Press) and was a finalist for the Colorado Book Award, and her second collection of poetry, *Trembling in the Bones*—about the Colorado Coal strike of 1913 and the 1914 Ludlow Massacre—was reissued in 2013 (3: A Taos Press). Her third poetry collection is *Memory's Rooms* (Conundrum Press). She is also a fiction writer who has published a novel and two collections of short stories. Her second collection, *Exiles and Expatriates*, won the 2014 Press Americana Prize. She mentors incarcerated men at the Sterling, Colorado, Correctional Facility, and she regularly reads from her work in the Denver metro area.

Title Index

S

T

V

W

First Line Index

I

L

O

R

S

T